꽃과 아내
Flowers and my wife
3

정송전 한영시집

Korean-English Poems Collection of Jeong Song Jeon

을지출판공사

■ 자서自序

　삶의 다양한 모습과 고단한 숨결이 시의 눈을 틔우고 오만 가지 허드레 잡념까지도 내게로 와서 시가 되었을 때, 그것은 돌올한 내 시의 성취라면 성취라고 감히 자부한다.
　나는 내 시집 〈내 이렇게 살다가〉의 자서에 다음과 같이 적은 적이 있다.
　'나의 여정은 분명 저녁나절쯤이지만 나의 시는 아직 새벽이다. 그래서 하염없이 회안에 젖는다.'
　내 삶이 어느 날 느닷없이 내가 아닌 것처럼 비춰지기도 했으며 삶의 질곡이 부질없이 그리움으로 다가오기도 했음을 고백한다. 그러나 그럴 때마다 내 삶의 심지를 곧추세우는 의연한 '여유'가 나를 건져 내기도 했다. 이것이 내 시의 이력이자 본령이라는 것을 나는 잊지 않는다.
　끝으로, 이 영문시집 펴내는데 있어 아내(신미자)와 아들(정주헌) 노고가 컸음을 밝혀 둔다.

　　　　　　　2022. 5. 10

　　　　　　　　　　지은이 정송전

■ The Preface of the Poet

When the various aspects and the weary breath of life put forth a bud of poetry and even tens of thousands of miscellaneous trivia thoughts come to me and become poetry, if I can call it, I dare to say that's the accomplishment of my outstanding poetry.

I once wrote the following in my essay for my collection of poems, 〈Living like this〉.

'My journey is certainly about the evening, but my poem is still dawn. So, I get soaked in endless remorse.'

I confess that one day my life suddenly felt like it wasn't me, and that life's ordeal came to me in vain longing. But every time that happened, the resolute 'Composure' that made my life upright, saved me. I do not forget that this is the history and the original characteristic of my poetry.

To conclude, I would like to acknowledge the efforts of my wife (Mija Shin) and son (Jooheon Jeong) in writing this English poem collection.

2022. 5. 10

Author Jeong Song jeon

차례

- 자서自序 The Preface of the Poet · 2
- 저자 약력 · 172

제1부 돌아올 수 없는 것들이 어디 세월뿐이던가
Part 1 Time is not the only thing that cannot be returned

어떤 이야기 A certain story / 10
어떤 꿈 A certain dream / 12
어느 날마다 Every day / 14
내 자리의 하늘 The sky in my seat / 16
꿈결에 · 1 In a dream · 1 / 18
꿈결에 · 2 In a dream · 2 / 20
이런 날은 In this day / 22
같은 하늘 아래서 · 1 Under the same sky · 1 / 24
같은 하늘 아래서 · 2 Under the same sky · 2 / 26
열중熱中 Enthusiasm / 28
꿈속에서 In the dream / 30
어느 날의 초상 A portrait of one day / 32
그림자 속에 In the shadow / 34
바닷가에서 At the beach / 36
꽃과 아내 Flowers and my wife / 38
늦가을 소묘 The sketch of late autumn / 42

———————————————————— Table of ontents

제 2 부 돌아오지 않는 것을 위하여
Part 2 For the things that never returned

지난날 The last days / 46

산울림은 The mountain echo is / 48

꽃인 줄 모르고 Unknowing itself as a flower / 50

가을 문턱 The threshold of autumn / 52

아지랑이가 Haze is / 54

장미 꽃말 The flower language of rose / 56

꽃을 두고 Putting the flower in front of me / 58

잡초는 Weeds are / 60

우듬지로 살자구나 Let's live as a treetop / 64

그대에게 To you / 66

그림자 드리우고 Casting a shadow / 68

목련은 A magnolia is / 70

땅에서 하늘로 From the ground to the sky / 72

사랑의 말 · 1 Words of love · 1 / 74

사랑의 말 · 2 Words of love · 2 / 76

그리움 일어 Rising the longing / 78

철마에게 To an iron horse / 82

차례

제3부 땅에서의 안부가 하늘에서의 기도로
Part 3 From the ground's regards to the sky's prayer

밤을 밝힌다 Lighting up the night / 88
가을에는 · 1 In autumn · 1 / 90
가을에는 · 2 In autumn · 2 / 92
바닷가 정경 The landscape of seaside / 94
가을빛 들면 When the autumn light enters / 96
단풍나무 아래서 Under the maple tree / 98
나를 정리하며 Organizing me / 100
섬에게 To an island / 102
수평선 · 1 The horizon line · 1 / 104
수평선 · 2 The horizon line · 2 / 106
가르치고 배우며 Teaching and learning / 108
구름바람 너머 하늘이 The sky over the cloudy wind is / 110
겨울 해변 풍경 The landscape of winter seaside / 114
기다림이 남기고 간 언어 The language that the wait left behind / 116
소식을 마중하며 Greeting the news / 118
제 모습 찾기 Finding myself / 122
겨울나무를 대신하여 On behalf of the winter tree / 124
달밤의 환영 Moon night hallucination / 126

Table of ontents

제4부 사랑과 이별의 물수제비뜨기
Part 4 The skipping stones of love and farewell

임에게 To my beloved / 132

너에게 To you / 134

양지동 소묘·1 Yangji-dong Sketch·1 / 136

양지동 소묘·2 Yangji-dong Sketch·2 / 138

양지동 소묘·3 Yangji-dong Sketch·3 / 140

코스모스 A cosmos / 142

꿈 속 In a dream / 144

꽃이 피어나는 이유 The reason why flowers bloom / 146

꽃씨 속 하늘 The sky inside a floral seed / 140

길에서 On the road / 150

거울 속 풍경 The scenery in the mirror / 152

정착지 A settlement area / 154

어떤 기다림 A certain wait / 156

어둠 속의 꿈 A dream in the dark / 158

그림자 하나·2 One shadow·2 / 162

내 이렇게 혼자서 I'm alone like this / 164

언제나 봄날의 모습으로 Always in the springtime / 166

꽃잎처럼 Like petals / 170

제 1 부 Part 1

돌아올 수 없는 것들이 어디 세월뿐이던가
Time is not the only thing that cannot be returned

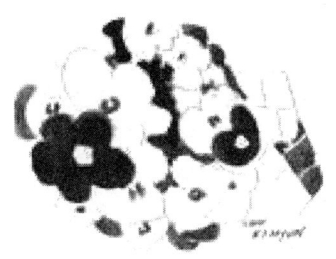

아직도 헷갈리는 것은
노란 꽃잎 속에
손에 잡힐 듯
내가 서 있나 보다.
- 「꽃과 아내」 중에서

What's still confusing,
In the yellow petals
Within her grasp
I guess I've been standing.
-The part of 「Flowers and my wife」

어떤 이야기

어느 누구에게
네 안부 묻느니

나는 그냥
꿈길로 살아야 하는가.

A certain story

To someone
Rather than I ask your news

Just do I
Have to live on a dream road?

어떤 꿈

우리가 갇힌 밀실

무지개 걸어놓고

서로 마주하는 몸짓

그리고 소리 없는 대화.

A certain dream

The secret room where we're locked in

Hanging a rainbow,

Gestures facing each other

And a voiceless conversation.

어느 날마다

보일 듯 외딴
빈 집
너울진 장독대에
노란 장다리 피어나면

가슴 헤집어
새겨 둔 촉감을
오늘도 쓰다듬는다.

별들은 이슬 속으로
내려와 사라진다.

조금씩 사위어가는 여백자락마다
손길이 닿는 삭신을 쓰다듬어
몸서리친 흔적

죽을 각오로 살면서
나의 이름 붙여보면
옷깃에 어룽진 메아리.

Every day

A vague and isolated
Empty house
On the spread platform for food jars
When the yellow flower of cabbage blooms

Stirring my chest
The engraved touch
Stroking it today again.

The stars descend and disappear
Into the dew.

At every dying margins little by little
After stroking the aches of the body with touches of
hands
Traces of shuddering body

Living at the risk of my life
If I name myself,
The echo that is variegated on the collar.

내 자리의 하늘

무언가 되돌려 주고

내 자리에 허허로이 남아

한 입 베어 머금은 하늘.

The sky in my seat

Giving something back

Left futilely on my seat

A sky with holding a bite.

꿈결에 · 1

뒤숭숭한 꿈결에
풀밭으로 나와
풀꽃과 마주한다.

조용히 그 자리에 자리 잡는다.
지금 나에겐 모두가
이상한 일뿐이다.

그림자가 이슬에 젖어
중량을 가중시키고
나의 그리움은
향방을 잃어버린다.

나는 다시금 꿈의 길섶에서
밤이 새도록 염원을 날리고
그대를 부르리.
그대를 만나보리.

In a dream · 1

In an uneasy dream
Coming out to the grass
I face the grass flowers.

I sit there quietly.
Everything to me now
It's just weird.

The shadow is wet with dews,
Adding its weight and
My longing
Have lost the direction.

On the roadside of a dream, once again
I've been all night long flying my wishes and
I will call you.
I will meet you.

꿈결에 · 2

마당에 서 있는 나무가
나를 붙잡고
절벽으로 떨어져 내리는 장면이다.

내 꿈을 대신 꾸어주는 몫으로
빈 몸으로 나앉아
밤을 뒤척이다가
얼레에 감긴
지난날의 자유로부터
어둠 속을 잠행한다.

자유라는 규격에 갇혀있는 나에게
누가 바람이 되어
내 말을 해줄는지.

침묵으로 덮어둔
빛과 향기를 되살려
어둠의 껍질을 벗기면
그대로 빛을 내다가
밤은
온갖 떠도는 시름을 묻는다.

In a dream · 2

The tree standing in the yard
Holds on to me,
Falls to a cliff, it's the scene.

As a share in making my dreams instead of me
Sitting out with an empty body,
After tossing and turning the night
From the freedom of the past
Which is rolled on a reel,
I travel in disguise into the dark.

To me, who I am locked in the standard as freedom
Who becomes the wind and
Will say about me?

Covered with silence
Reviving the light and the scent
If peeling the dark skin,
It shines as it is and
The night
Buries all kinds of floating worries.

이런 날은

아침이 오는 벼랑으로
햇살이 날려

허물고 허물어도 쌓이는 말
어쩌면 남겨둔 흔적일 거다.

시선이 닿는 곳마다
늘 하늘거리는 모습으로
모든 것이 영롱해진다.

저녁 늦은 시간에
모여 앉아
몇 차례이고
세월을 가늠해 보지만
우리는 모두가 잠깐
머물다 가는 풍경으로 남는다.

In this day

Toward the cliff where the morning comes
Sunshine blows

Words are stacked even after breaking down and breaking down,
That could be a trace left behind.

Wherever the gaze reaches,
Always with a shape of swaying
Everything becomes brilliant.

Late in the evening
Seated together
Several times even
Guessing the years,
We all remain
As a scenery of staying and going just a moment.

같은 하늘 아래서 · 1

같은 하늘 아래 살면서도
사는 세상이 다르지 않는가.
세상이 다르게 사는 건지
세상을 다르게 사는 건지
누가 생각이나 했겠는가.

자기 몫으로
누구든지 어디서 무엇을 하느냐가
같은 세상에 다른 삶이 아니겠는가.

아무 것도 내세울 게 없이
내 흘러간 세월
창 밖을 내다보면서
죽음을 예견하고 살아오느라
여기까지 떠밀려 살아왔다.

힘에 부치게 사는 이들
낮춘 처신이기에
독한 세상만은 아니더라.

Under the same sky · 1

Even though living under the same sky,
Isn't the world living different?
Whether the world lives differently or
Living the world differently,
No one would have thought of it.

On its share
Whoever does where and what,
It could be different living in the same world.

Without anything to show off
My passing years
Looking out the window,
By living with the premonition of death
I have been pushed to live to this point.

Those whose lives are too much for them
Because of low behavior,
The world was not just severe.

같은 하늘 아래서 · 2

적막을 휘저어
눈에 익은 산과 들이
차창을 열고 들어온다.

하루하루 사는 거야
제 잔병을 잊고 사는 법이다.

하룻내 두통이 설치다가 사라지고
새삼 나는 하늘 위로 떠오른다.

가고 오는 계절이 팔에 안긴다.
잠결에 다짐한 우리의 결속
무엇인가, 흐릿한 안개로 알 수가 없다.

깜박 잊고 지낸 손바닥에
꼭 쥔 과일
사랑의 유산이다.

Under the same sky · 2

Stirring the silence
The familiar mountain and the field
Open the car window and enter.

Living day after day,
It's the way to forget about our minor illness.

My headache had raged then disappeared within one day
Newly I rise over the sky.

The passing and coming seasons throw themselves in my arms.
Our unity that is promised during dreaming
Something, can't be known by the dim fog.

In my palm that I had forgotten
The fruit with holding tightly
It's the heritage of love.

열중熱中

사람이 바라보는 게 무엇일까,

바람이며 구름 따라

귓속을 열어 놓고 들으렷다.

Enthusiasm

What's it that a person is watching?

Along with the wind and the clouds

Listen to that with opening the inner ear.

꿈속에서

잊혀진 나날 끝머리
아련히 멀어진 모습을 본다.

그 시간은 지금
삭은 넝쿨을 타고
허물어진 흙담을 오른다.

지워버리고만 싶은
내 유년의 언덕에서
이날토록 키워온 말씨들이
눈을 뜨고 빛난다.

불면의 깊은 시간에
꿈속에서 돌아누워
팔랑개비로 맴돈다.

In the dream

The end part of forgotten days
I see the figure that is fading away afar.

That time is now
Rides with a rotten vine,
Climbs a destroyed dirt wall.

I just want to erase
The words that I have been raised until this day
On the hill of my childhood
It shines with opening the eyes.

In the deep hours of sleeplessness
Lying down in my dreams,
Hovering around like a pinwheel.

어느 날의 초상

지금도 간이역 마당에
서성이고 있을까.

체념으로 익힌 시절의 하나하나가
모질게 유산으로 남는다.

거품으로 나앉아
예감하지 못했던 나를 찾는다.

한 다발 묶은 그리움은
영상 속에서 흔들린다.

모두가
어둠에 삭아 내린다.

살다보면 누구라도
뒷자리는 저 만치 아름다운 것일 테지.

A portrait of one day

Even now, in the yard of a way station
Would it be hanging around?

Each one of the years I've learned from resignation,
Remains harshly as a heritage.

Sitting out as bubbles
Find me who I didn't have a premonition.

Longing tied like a bundle
Are swaying in the video.

All are
Descending after decaying by the dark.

Anyone in their life
The remained place might be as beautiful as that much.

그림자 속에

노을 뒷켠
시선 머물었던 자리에
침묵의 소리

언약을 남긴
속 속의 눈빛이며 눈물이
그림자가 되는가.

비로소 그림자가
달빛을 타고 피어오르더니
바다를 출렁이게 한다.

외풍 센 방에 홀로 앉아
까맣게 잊었던 그림자를 그린다.

푯말로 박힌
나는 지금 어디에 있는가.
그림자 속 어디쯤 있는가.

In the shadow

Behind the sunset
Where eye glances stayed
The sound of silence

Remaining a covenant,
Inside the eyes and the tears
Could it become a shadow?

Finally, the shadow
Rising as riding in the moonlight,
Makes the sea float.

Sitting alone in the strong windy room
Missing my shadow that is forgotten completely.

Being stuck as a signpost
Where am I now?
Where am I in a shadow?

바닷가에서

저 바다는 언제나
마저 못한 말을 지녔음이라

하늘과 바람이
수평선에 서서
바다의 말을 듣는다.

세상의 모든 일이
별빛일 순 없겠지.

언제쯤
저 바다의 말이
내 귀에도 들릴는지.

바닷가에서
가슴팍으로 질러오는 파도와
시간을 보내다가
내 빈 자리로 돌아온다.

At the beach

The sea is always
Might have a word that couldn't finish

The sky and the wind
Standing on the horizon,
Listen to the word of the sea.

All the worldly things
Could not be starlight.

When,
That sea's word,
Can I hear it in my ear also?

At the beach
With the waves rushing through my chest
Spending my times,
I come back to my empty seat.

꽃과 아내

별 말이 없던 아내가
아침 햇살을 제치고
아파트 잔디밭을 내다보며
'여보, 여기 노란 꽃이 참 예뻐요'
오랜만에 감동을 건넨다.

갱년기라, 입을 꼭 다문 미망이더니
아내의 화면 전체가 꽃이다.

시력도 좋지 않은 아내가 바라본 꽃은
꽃이 아니라 자기였을지 모르지.

아직도 헷갈리는 것은
노란 꽃잎 속에
손에 잡힐 듯
내가 서 있나 보다.

이 밤엔 무엇을 사위어
저 하늘을 휘어 날려 볼까.
나보다 꽃으로 한 깨침이겠지.

Flowers and my wife

My wife, who didn't say much
Out of the morning sun
Looking out over the lawn of the apartment
 'Honey, the yellow flowers are so pretty'
It's been a long time to send me an impression.

Owing to menopause, have drifted with unspoken state
Now my wife's whole screen is a flower.

My wife, who has poor eyesight, looked at the flowers
Maybe it was herself, not the flower.

What's still confusing,
In the yellow petals
Within her grasp
I guess I've been standing.

What can it burn up at this night and
Can be blown away lightly over the sky?
It would be enlightenment by a flower than me.

자정 무렵, 창밖의 불빛이 포근하여 내다보니
노란 꽃이 모두 없어졌다.
'여보, 꽃들이 모두 어디로 가버렸어'
놀란 소리에 아내가 다가와
'낮에 애들이 몰려다니더니 모두 꺾어가 버렸네.'

그렇지, 무엇인가 다짐으로
푸르름 그대로 놔두고
한 가닥 바람으로 나를 날린다.

About midnight, the light outside the window was so warm that I looked out
All the yellow flowers are gone.
'Honey, all the flowers were gone'
My wife came up to me at the sound of surprise.
'The kids were swarming around in the day and they picked all away.'

Yes, with the determination of something
Leaving it green,
Blowing me with a gust of wind.

늦가을 소묘

꽃밭에 하늘이 가득하다.
손바닥에 몇 낱의 씨앗을 고른다.

손길 닿는 시간이면
아직 묻어나는 바람소리.

씨앗의 날개엔
부름을 듣는 귀가 있다.

밤에도 씨앗은 달음질로
하늘을 달린다.

마지막 햇살을 받으며
씨앗을 고르고 있다.
아직도 넉넉한 시간이다.

The sketch of late autumn

The sky is full in the flower field.
Picking a few seeds in my palm.

When it's the time with touching of hand,
The sound of the wind is still attached.

In the wings of seed
There's an ear of hearing the calling.

Even at night, the seed
Runs in a rush through the sky.

Receiving the last sunshine
I choose the seeds.
It's still enough time.

제 2 부 Part 2

돌아오지 않는 것을 위하여
For the things that never returned

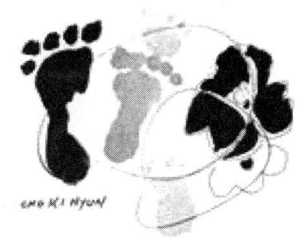

그래, 오늘은 너같이 살고
내일은 나같이 살지.

사람의 말이
어쩌면 이렇게도 어처구니없을까.
- 「사랑의 말 · 2」 중에서

Yes, I live like you today and
Will live like me tomorrow.

A human's word is,
How could it be absurd like this?
- The part of 「Words of love · 2」

지난날

눈바람 속
잎새 진 자리에
열꽃으로 남아서

나 그대로
그대와 동행하여

여기까지 지켜 온
세월의 고비였을 뿐이었다.

The last days

In blizzard
At the spot of falling leaves
Remaining as a fire flower

As I am
Along with you

Kept up to here,
It was just a crisis moment of the years.

산울림은

부소산성에 오르다.

"백마강 달밤에 물새가 울어"
누가 자연을 그려 놓았는가.

고란사의 풍경소리
낙화암의 비명소리
노을이 눈을 맞춰준다.

사랑하는 것 모두 서성거리다가
공허한 바람에 빨려 들어가

무슨 소리가 빗소리에 젖어
무엇 하나 지탱하지 못하고
불 먹은 쇠로
혼자 남는가.

The mountain echo is

I climb on the Buso Fortress.

"A waterfowl cries on the moon night at Baekma River"
Who painted nature?

The sound of scenery in Goran Temple
The screaming sound of Nakhwa Rock
The sunset meets its eyes.

All the loving things are hanging around,
Sucked into by the empty winds

What sound does it get wet in the rain sound and
Can't it sustain anything and
As iron by eating fire
Has it remained alone?

꽃인 줄 모르고

이슬 속 내비치는 하늘을 본다.
눈망울 굴리는 아침에
수줍음 타는 몸짓이 곱다.

해맑은 새벽에
이슬로 환상하는
숨결 소리.

무지개가 선 기슭에
꽃은 꽃인 줄 모르고
요정들의 옷을 입힌다.

기어이 너는
나의 내부로 들어와
바람을 놓고 갔다.

웃음 짓는 여유와 자랑으로
나를 다시 마중해 다오.

고개 숙인 머리맡으로
내가 이렇게 왔다.

Unknowing itself as a flower

I see the sky shining through the dew
In the morning with rolling eyes
The gesture of shyness is pretty.

At the dawn when the sun is bright
Transforming as dew
It's breathing sound.

At the shore when the rainbow stands
The flower doesn't know itself as a flower,
It puts clothes on fairies.

Finally, you
Came to my inner side,
Left after putting the wind.

With smiling relaxation and proud
Please come out to meet me again.

Beneath of your drooping head
I come like this.

가을 문턱

장다리 대궁이
연보라 분을 바르고
봄날을 다 차지하더니

바람이 다가와
문지방에 앉으며
연지분 씻으라 하네.

세상 사는 것들은
파도로 출렁거리네.

가뭄이랑 태풍을
한 숨에 둘러 앉혔네.

아무래도 무엇인가
할 말이 남아 있나 보네.

꽃잎 속으로 잠적했다가
단물을 빨아올리는 햇살에
묻지 않아도 대답하고
하늘에 걸린 가을 낮달을
한 입 베어 무네.

The threshold of autumn

The stalk of cabbage flowers
Puts on lilac powder on its face,
Occupied the whole spring and

The wind comes and
Sitting at the threshold,
Asking it to wash the lilac powder.

The things that live in the world,
Is waving by waves.

Drought and typhoon
Were seated around at a burst.

Somehow something,
There may be left to say.

Vanished into the petals and
To the sunshine that sucks up the sweet water,
Answer it without asking and
With the moon on a day that hung in the sky,
Take a cutting bite.

아지랑이가

앙심을 품고 있다가
없는 말 지껄이더니
포박하러 달려든다.

가슴 내려앉던 것
시치미를 떼고
노을 속의 나는
바람을 희롱한다.

잘 가세요, 도련님
눈물 머금고 손짓하여도
구름은 언제나 하늘 언저리에 남아있는 것.

한나절 혼자서
꿈속의 손길 잡고 있다가
눈부신 신부新婦로 변장한다.

그대 그림자에 눕는다.
아직도 거들떠보지 못한 최후가
천지에 가득 퍼져 오른다.

Haze is

Holding with a grudge and
Chatting meaningless words,
Rushing for capturing.

What it descended into my heart
Pretending to unknowing
In the sunset glow, I am,
Teasing the wind.

Goodbye, Young Master
Even though gesturing hands with tears
Clouds always remain around the sky.

Half a day alone
Holding hands of the dream,
Disguise as a dazzling bride.

Lying down on your shadow.
The last moment that doesn't pay attention until now
Spreads and rises all over the world.

장미 꽃말

장미 안섶의 이야길 누가 알겠는가.

알아들을 수 없는 말로
나를 불러 놓고
되레 남의 일같이 바라보기만 한다.

그윽하기 만한 향기
얼마나 그리던 환영인가.

오늘도 한 송이 너를
하염없이 들여다본다.

자기 모순의 아픔도 이겨 내고
되살아난 환생이겠지.

The flower language of rose

Who knows the story inside the jacket of rose?

With incomprehensible words
Calls me in and
Just looks at me as if it's other's business.

Only a subtle fragrance
How much did I yearn for its phantom?

Today again, a piece of you
I look into endlessly.

Overcoming the pain of self-contradiction,
It must be a reincarnation.

꽃을 두고

태양을 두고
오늘 하루도 다짐이었다.

언제부턴지
직관보다 관능이 화려한 체질

환상을 떠올려
공중에 나를 올려놓고 함성을 질러댄다.

어쩌자고 그토록
진공의 나를 불러대는가.

고요한 것
퇴색한 것
바람과 구름도 모두
너와 함께 잡혀 있다.

Putting the flower in front of me

Putting the sun in front of me
Today was also a resolution.

Since when is it,
A constitution more splendid sensuality than intuition

Recalling the fantasy
Putting me in the air and shouting.

For what reason to such an extent
Calling me out from the vacuum?

The silent one
The faded one
Both the wind and the clouds are
Captivated with you.

잡초는

들녘이 폭우에 씻겨 맨살로 누웠다.
장마가 그치고 몇 날이 지나
하늘 한 자락 잡아당겨 무지개를 만들어
흙살이 패인 들녘에 온통
기운차게 잡초가 자라고 있었다.

땅 속에 한세월 묻혀 있으면서도
영양분을 사용하지 않고 지내고
생리대사도 변화하여 살아남는다.
아무리 광합성을 한다기로니
그 어떤 재앙에도 살아남을 수 있게끔
진화된 잡초여.

손바닥만 한 토양 중에 수만 낟알의 잡초 종자가
오랜 기간 자생하는 근성을
내 어찌 모르고 살아왔는가.

돌 틈새에 손을 들어올리는
명아주 소리쟁이 질경이 달맞이꽃
몇 만 년의 환생인가.

Weeds are

The field was washed away in heavy rain and laid bare.
A few days after the rainy season ended
Pulling a part of the sky and make a rainbow
All over the field where soil skin is carved in,
Weeds were growing vigorously.

Even though it has been buried in the ground for years
Without using nutrients
Physiological metabolism also changes and survives.
No matter how much photosynthesis is done,
To survive any catastrophe
Evolved weeds!

Tens of thousands of weed seeds in the palm-sized soil
The temper that grows independently for a long time
How did I live without knowing?

Raising its hand in a stone crevice
A goosefoot, a Rumex Crispus, a plantain, and an evening primrose
How many tens of thousands of years of reincarnation?

한여름 지난 지금
남들은 꽃을 떨구고 가을을 담고 있는데
너는 이제 봄이라
언제 꽃피워 가을을 익히려는가.

바람으로 다가가 지켜본다.
신통하지, 시간을 앞당겨 그새 꽃피워 놓았다.
그렇지, 삶은 그토록 아름다운 것이구나.
이슬 묻은 소리쟁이 종자는
날갯짓으로 강물을 타고 흐른다.
도깨비바늘이 우리 집에까지 들어왔다.
새삼 신기한 감동이다.

언젠가는 땅 속에 들어가서
나도 휴면할 수 있을까
자신의 힘으로 존재할 수 있을까.

오늘밤
스스로 묻고 대답하느라 새벽을 맞는다.

Now, after a midsummer
Others drop flowers and contain autumn, but
You are now spring,
When will you bloom and want to ripen autumn?

Approaching as the wind and watching.
It's marvelous, it has blossomed by pulling time.
Right, life is so beautiful.
The dewy seed of Rumex Crispus,
Flows through the river with its wings.
A Spanish needles came into even our house.
It is a newly strange impression.

Someday I will go into the ground,
Can I be dormant too?
Can I exist with my own strength?

Tonight
I meet the dawn as asking and answering myself.

우듬지로 살자구나

흘러가는 시간에
다시 돌아올 수 없는 시절과
하냥 가슴 내려앉아
서성이며 서 있다가

그림자 따라
흩어져 있는 것 살아
무슨 영상으로 피어나는가.
어둠이 소리 없이 내려와
나를 기다리게 하고 있다.

남아 있는 앙금을 지금 날려버릴 순 없을까.
서로의 형상을 마주할 수 있는 거리에서
깊이 바라볼 일이다.
새롭게 다가오는 시절
뿌리를 박고 우듬지로 살자구나.

Let's live as a treetop

At the flowing time
Irreversible days and
Heart come down together
Strolling around and standing

Following the shadow
Living what is scattered,
What kind of image does it bloom with?
The dark descends voicelessly,
It makes me wait.

Can I blow away the remaining grudges now?
At a distance that we can face each other's shape,
It's the case of looking deeply.
The newly approaching years,
Let's live as a treetop putting down roots.

그대에게

보고 싶을 때
꽃대인 듯
그림자가 기대선다.

일그러진 그림자는
어디로 돌아갔을까.
지난 일은
흐릴수록 아름답기만 하다.

잊었다 싶을 때
슬며시 돌아와
서 있는 그대.

To you

When I miss you,
As if it's a flower stalk,
The shadow leans against.

The twisted shadow is
Where did it go back?
The past story is
The vaguer it is, just the more beautiful it is.

When I seem to forget,
Secretly coming back,
You are standing.

그림자 드리우고

오늘도 그림자와 동행하며
말을 잃고
지금은 뒤척이는 밤이다.

내 지내온 굽이는
억지를 부려온 나날 같기만 했다.

부푼 꿈의 너울 안으로
무슨 기억을 쓸어내고 있는 걸까.

뿌리 없는 나무의 어지러움을 달래다가
돌아앉아 염언念言을 외우고
나는 다시 떠나야 한다.

끝나지 않은 그리움
그림자는 마냥 드리우고
그 소용돌이 안으로
별이 여울진다.

Casting a shadow

Even today, along with my shadow
Lost my words
Now it's a tossing and turning night.

My past ups and downs,
It was like the days of making an unreasonable demand.

In a heaving sea of swelling dreams
What memories am I sweeping away?

Soothing the dizziness of a rootless tree,
Turning my back and memorizing the word of deep thought then
I must leave again.

The endless longing
The shadow is always hanging and
Into the swirling
The star enters roughly.

목련은

애초부터 사랑과
이별을 터득하고

밤새 소복으로 치장한
미망의 여인.

A magnolia is

From the beginning, love and
Farewell, understands it and

Decorated with white mourning clothes all night long
A widow.

땅에서 하늘로

먼 산을 바라보다가
빈 하늘 한 자락에
햇살 날려 바위에 부딪는 것
젊은 날의 그리움이었다.

그 숱한 꿈
앙상한 뿌리로 비탈에 서 있는가.

구름은 호수를 건너고
내가 구름을 헤치고
구름은 가까이 자욱하기만 하다.

이슬로 다가와 구겨버리는
풍경을 머리맡에 눕히고
산이 하는 말을 들어야지
거스름이 없는 말을 귀담아 들으며
먼 산에 그려진
나를 그린 산이 아닌가.

From the ground to the sky

Looking at the far mountain
In the edge of an empty sky
What crashes to the rock by blowing sunshine is,
That's the longing for youth.

Those plentiful dreams,
Do they stand on the slope with skinny roots?

Clouds cross the lake and
I push my way through the clouds and
The clouds are closely dense.

The scenery that approaches as dew and crumples
I lay down it my bedside and
I will hear what the mountain says,
Listening to the word without any objection
What is painted on the far mountain is,
Is it the mountain that painted me?

사랑의 말 · 1

벼랑으로 몰려 와
심연深淵에 추락하는 나.

잊을 수도 있었고
잊을 수도 없었던 꿈결에

가위눌림 속
나는 그 어디다가 대고
무어라 발설할 수가 없구나.

Words of love · 1

Rushing to the cliff,
Falling into the abyss. I am,

Could have forgotten,
In an unforgettable dream

During paralyzing nightmare
Nowhere I can
Disclose my word.

사랑의 말 · 2

화병에 꽂힌 안개꽃
마주 보다가

이슬 내리던 새벽
아득한 꿈길로 들어선다.

그래, 오늘은 너같이 살고
내일은 나같이 살지.

사람의 말이
어쩌면 이렇게도 어처구니없을까.

Words of love · 2

Gypsophila in the vase
Looking face to face

When it's dawn with falling dew,
Going in a way of a dim dream.

Yes, I live like you today and
Will live like me tomorrow.

A human's word is,
How could it be absurd like this?

그리움 일어

두통이 멎은 뒤라
언 손을 입김으로 녹이며
달빛에 잠든 강을 바라보았다.
강바람이 가까이 다가와
가슴을 열어 준다.

언제부턴가 까닭 없이 돌아앉은
그 침묵의 벼랑 속에서
아직은 그런 대로의 모습으로
강을 잠재운 달빛에
그리움 일어

어디론가 일상은 달려가는데
헛눈 파는 사이
강바람은 사념을 체념한다.

높지도 않은 중심을 기어오르면
하늘과 땅이 뒤엉키는 허상이여.

Rising the longing

After ending of headache
Melting in my frozen hands with mouth breath
I see the sleeping river by moonlight.
The river wind comes closer and
Opens its chest.

Seated around motivelessly from someday
In the cliff of that silence
Still, as it is,
Due to the moonlight that calmed the river
Rising the longing

Ordinary life is running somewhere,
During taking my eyes off
The river wind gives up its thoughts.

Crawling up the center that is not even high,
Tangled with the sky and the ground, the illusion it is.

오늘이 헐린 자리에
지친 팔다리를 늘어뜨리고 서서
허물을 벗어버리자.
혹시라도 가슴 속에 남아 있는
맥을 짚어 잠들게 하자.

The place where today is demolished,

Standing with stretching out tired arms and legs

Let's throw away the skin.

Might be left in my mind,

Let's feel the pulse and put it to sleep.

철마에게
— 임진각에서

녹슨 철마가 하늘에 시선을 놓고
구름이 되었다가
바람이 되었다가
할 말을 잊어버렸다.

잠을 어떻게 잘 수 있겠는가.
꿈도 꿀 게 없겠다.

눈에 밟히는 어느 한 가지도
외면하고 살 수는 없겠지,
달빛이 별들을 불러내어
강둑에 모닥불을 피워놓고
하늘로 튀어 오르던 불티를 검잡던
이웃들이 제 깜냥껏 사는 모습이다.

임진강에서 문산으로
파주에서 금촌으로
홍수가 범람하고 있어도
삭은 세월을 안고 몸부림치지만
발목이 저려 주저앉아 있는가.

To an iron horse
- At Imjingak Pavilion

A rusty iron horse giving its eyes to the sky
Becomes clouds
Becomes the winds,
Forgot what to say.

How could it sleep?
It might have nothing to dream.

Anything that is attracted to the eyes
It could not live with turning away its face,
The moonlight calls out the stars,
Having a bonfire on the riverbank
Grabbing the flying fire flake to the sky,
It's the appearance of neighbors' living within their ability.

From Imjin River to Munsan
From Paju to Geumchon
Even if the flood is overflowing,
Struggled with holding rotten years, but
Are you sitting down due to the numbness in your ankle?

깨어나라
무슨 수작을 부려서라도.

망초대궁에 발목이 잡혀 있는 기차가
간밤엔 헛바퀴만 굴리고 있었다
이상한 일이야.

이제라도 하얀 연기 뿜으며
향수의 기적을 울려라.

흐린 불빛 속 차창에 어리는
오뉘의 그림자 다시 한 번 보자.

Wake up
At all costs.

The train that is captivated its ankle by the stalk of a
Glauber salt,
Was rolling useless wheels in the last night
It's a weird thing.

Even from now, letting out white smoke,
Whistle your horn of nostalgia.

Flickering on its window in the faint light,
Let's see again the shadow of brother and sister.

제3부 Part 3

땅에서의 안부가 하늘에서의 기도로
From the ground's regards to the sky's prayer

저승으로 지고 갈
너무나 작고 초라한 나를
하늘 빈자리에 남겨두면 어떤가.

언제나 풋풋한 그 하늘
세월마저 안가고 맴돌면 어쩌나
- 「나를 정리하며」 중에서

Will carry it on my back to the afterlife
So small and humble me
How about leaving it in the spare place of the sky?

Ever fresh sky
What if even the years don't leave and are lingering there?
-The part of 「Organizing me」

밤을 밝힌다

목롯집에서 흘리던 신소리
눈 쌓인 어깨를 들썩이며
거리로 나와
밤을 보듬었다.

밤이 깊을수록
지내온 날이 자꾸만 되돌아 보이고 밟혀

꿈속에서
하얗게 밤을 밝힌다.

Lighting up the night

Making a joke at the small bar
Moving my snowy shoulders
Coming out to the street,
I hugged the night.

The deeper the night
The past days repeatedly have been seen in my mind,

In my dream
I am lighting up the night wholly.

가을에는 · 1

햇살이 이슬에 젖다가
풀잎 끝에
아침을 맞는다.

벌레도 숨어드는
가을 언덕에서
마지막 과일들이 익는다.

이 가을은 누구에게로 갔다가
누구에게로 오는지
알 수 없는 시간이다.

청명하기만 한 이 계절
나는 허공에 가벼이 유영을 한다.

지금은
가늠 수 없는 빛으로 서서
맨 마지막 가을을 전별한다.

In autumn · 1

The sunlight is wet with dew then
At the end of the grass leaf
Meets the morning.

Even an insect hides
On the autumn hill,
The last fruits are ripe.

To whom this autumn goes,
To whom come back,
It's an incomprehensible time.

These clear one season
I lightly swim in the air.

Now
Standing with an irresistible light,
Giving a farewell party to the final autumn.

가을에는 · 2

가까운 산자락이
얼굴을 들어
가을 강물 속에서 떠오르네.

하늘만 남고
어디에도 그림자는 없네.

마당에 서성이는
마지막 햇볕을 쥐어보네.

가지마다 휘도록 매달린 무게
그 속 깊이엔
황금빛 씨알이 영글어 가득하네.

In autumn · 2

The part of the mountain nearby
Lifts its face,
Rises from in the autumn river.

Only the sky remains,
Nowhere its shadow is.

Strolling around in the yard
Grabbing that final sunshine.

The windingly hanging weight at each branch
That deep inside,
The golden seeds fully ripen.

바닷가 정경

오늘도 기우는 하루의 마감시간
바다를 채색한다.

아쉬움의 나날
흐린 거울 앞에서 매무새를 고치다가

시작도 끝도 없는 바다에 나앉아
하릴없이 굳어가는 표정.

나에겐 언제나
무서운 기다림의 끝이었다.

세상 모든 것 담아
하늘 가 공허 속으로 몰아넣는다.

달이 구름에 들어서고
그때 마침 얼비치는
나의 말.

서로가 흔적을 남긴 자리
꽃은 어디서나 홀로 핀다.

The landscape of seaside

At a tilting final time of today again
I paint the sea.

Regretful days,
Fixing the appearance of clothes in front of a blurry mirror

Coming out of the sea of no beginning and no end,
Aimlessly stiffening complexion.

Always for me,
It was the end of scary waiting.

Holding all the worldly things,
Driving into the void near the sky.

The moon enters in the clouds,
Just then, glimmering
My words.

Where each other left a mark,
Flowers always bloom alone everywhere.

가을빛 들면

요사이 졸음이 많아졌다.
힘 부치게 엄습해 오는 잠을 어쩌지 못하겠다.

가을빛 들면
전신엔 또렷한 의식이 가득 번진다.

피고 또 피어 휘날리는 갈꽃
모두들 원형으로 남겨둬라 한다.

내게는 아무런 까닭이 없고
다만 가을 하늘을 보려함이라.

무엇 때문에 하늘을 보려함인가.

When the autumn light enters

These days, I have much drowsiness.
Irresistibly I can't do anything to overwhelming sleeping.

When the autumn light enters,
The clear consciousness fully spread to the whole body.

Fluttering weed flowers blooming and blooming
Everybody says to leave it as an original form.

There's no reason for me
Just want to see the autumn sky.

For what reason do I want to see the sky?

단풍나무 아래서

그토록 푸르름이 단풍으로 얼비취는 것은

누구라도 삭혀온 세월의

고요한 굽이굽이이겠지.

Under the maple tree

All that greenery that turns into glimmering into autumn leaves

Of the years that anyone has soothed

It must be quiet ups and downs.

나를 정리하며

버리지 못하는 허물
담아 놓고 다시 덜어내어
입김으로 촉촉이 적시거나
다시 햇살에 말리며
알 수 없는 짓으로
나를 괴롭혀도
구름은 그저 유영할 뿐이다.

아직도 미지의 한 켠에
끓어오름으로 우두커니 서서
떠날 줄 모르는 얼굴.

저승으로 지고 갈
너무나 작고 초라한 나를
하늘 빈자리에 남겨두면 어떤가.

언제나 풋풋한 그 하늘
세월마저 안가고 맴돌면 어쩌나
지친 마음에
나뭇가지의 흔들림을 자기 탓으로 알면 어쩌나.

Organizing me

The exuviae that cannot be thrown away
Put it in and take it out again
Moisturizing wetly by the breath or
Dry it again with sunshine
By doing inexplicably,
Harass me, but
The clouds are merely swimming.

Still in one corner of the unknown,
Standing around boilingly
The face that cannot leave.

Will carry it on my back to the afterlife
So small and humble me
How about leaving it in the spare place of the sky?

Ever fresh sky
What if even the years don't leave and are lingering there?
With a weary mind
What if it blames itself for the swaying of the branches?

섬에게

언제나 안개에 파묻힌
섬.

바위에 쪼그리고 앉았다가
구름으로 달려가다가
바람으로 달려가다가

파도에 씻긴 그리움은
섬이다.

To an island

Always buried in the fog
The island.

Squatting down on a rock
Running to the clouds
Racing to the wind

The longing that is washed by the waves
It's an island.

수평선 · 1

한여름 바다가
하늘에 이르는 길을
무지개로 닦아 놓고

아무 말 없이
자기 형상 남겨 놓고

하늘로 출렁이며
바라보는 것은 무엇일까.

The horizon line · 1

The sea of midsummer is
The way to the sky,
Wiping it with a rainbow

Wordlessly
Leaving in its shape

Rocking into the sky
What does it look at?

수평선 · 2

안개 속 뱃고동소리가
다시 열리는 하루를
흔들어 깨운다.

수평선은 파도를 잠재우며
길을 터놓고
안개 속으로 돌아오지만
눈앞의 모두는 그대로다.

이 시간, 이 자리에선
구름이 바다가 되고
바다가 구름에 가득하다.

밤의 별빛은
수평선을 지워버리고
노을 속의 기억을 되살려
그리움을 날리게 한다.

The horizon line · 2

The boat horn in the fog,
A day that opens again
Awakens it with swaying.

The horizon puts the waves to sleep
Opens the road
Returns into the fog, but
Everything in front is the same.

This time, in this place
The clouds become the sea
The sea is full of clouds.

The starlight of the night
Erases the horizon
Evoking the memories in the sunset,
Makes the longing fly.

가르치고 배우며
−교장으로 취임하여

우리들의 시간 그 정오에
무엇이 될 수 있을까.

비록 더디게라도
꽃처럼 향기로울 것을 다짐하자.

흙 진실 가르치고 일깨운
세 번째 휘돌아 친 나이테
푸른 뜨락에 거목으로 자라나
그 어떤 보석으로 견줄 수 있으랴.

저 하늘 한 자락에
가르침마다 삶을 수놓아
큰 획을 긋기도 하겠지.

머물러 살고 싶은 마을에
이제 그 모습 교정의 그림자로 남아
다음 날의 모습을 그리워하리.

먼동을 앞세워 내달리는
우리들의 요람에서.

Teaching and learning
- Inaugurated as principal

Our time at that noon
What could we be?

Even if it's tardy,
Let's make up our mind to be fragrant like flowers.

Teaching and awakening the truth of soil
The annual rings of a tree with whirling around three times
Growing up like a great tree in the green yard
What kind of jewel can it compare to?

One edge of that sky
Embroidering life at every teaching,
Will mark a milestone.

In the village where we want to stay and live
Now remained as a shadow of the school yard,
Will miss the next day's figure.

Running behind the distant sun rising
In our cradle.

구름바람 너머 하늘이

아무것도 내세울 것 없는 나에게
너는 구름바람 너머 하늘이었지.
손에 잡힐 듯 서로 다가와
마음 주는 눈길을 내었지.
무엇 때문인지 지순한 순수까지도
거절할 수 없었지.

어느 날
네가 얼룩으로 치장된 것을 알았을 때
너에게 너무 쉬운 존재였음을
포기하기엔 많은 시간이 걸린다는 것을
땅거미가 일러주었지.

미안해요, 한마디 비음이 없었다면
아직도 너를 바라볼 수 있었을지.
어리석음을 되새김하면서
초라해 보이는 나이가 되면
나를 용서할 수 있을는지.

The sky over the cloudy wind is

To me who has nothing to show off,
You were the sky beyond the clouds wind.
Coming over as if grabbing each other in hand,
Had given each other eye with heart.
For what reason, even pure innocence
Couldn't refuse it.

One day
When I noticed you're decorated with stains,
It was too easy for you
It takes a long time to give up,
The twilight told me that.

I'm sorry. If there wasn't a word of nasal,
Still, whether I could look at you.
Reciting my foolishness
When the time of shabby age comes,
Wonder if I could forgive me.

거짓의 몸짓과 고백이여
두 번 다시 이유를 묻지 않았고
너 역시 핑계를 대지 않았지.
다시는 마음 가지 않으리라 결심은
문지방을 앞서 나서는 뒷모습을 바라보다
아무 생각도 못한 채 멍했었겠지.

저 하늘은
푸르게 빛나는 관능의 몸
언제나 머뭇대는 갈등이겠지.

False gesture and confession,
I didn't ask the reason never again and
You didn't give me an excuse.
The resolution that I will never open my mind,
Looking at the back appearance of going out ahead
of a threshold,
Might have a vacant mind thoughtlessly.

That sky is
A sensual body of shining blue,
It would be always a hesitating struggle.

겨울 해변 풍경

모래바람에 비슷이
한 무더기 해당화
파도소리 머금어
겨울나기라.

가시 촘촘히 앙상한 가지에
새 한 마리
체온 놓고 갔다.

연분홍꽃 진 자리에
아무도 들어주지 않은
겨울 바다의 비음.

The landscape of winter seaside

Obliquely by sandstorm
A bunch of Rugusa roses
Holding the sound of waves,
Might be a wintering.

On the bare branch with dense thorns
A bird
Had gone after leaving its body heat.

In the place of pale pink flower's falling
Nobody would listen to,
The nasal sound of the winter sea.

기다림이 남기고 간 언어

1
마침내
기다림과 동행은
차창 밖의 바람으로
그와는 무관한 타인이 되어 있다.

2
기다림 속에는
아직 못 잊은 스치움이
가득 담겨 있는 것.

3
기다림은 사랑만큼이나
어눌하지만
빛바랜 세월이
그에게도 끝나지 않음이다.

The language that the wait left behind

1

Finally

The wait and the accompanying

Due to the wind outside the window,

It became a stranger who has nothing to do with him.

2

In the wait

The grazing that has not yet been forgotten,

What it's filled with.

3

The wait is as much as love

Inarticulate but

Faded years are

Not finished to him either.

소식을 마중하며

어디로 가서
들꽃의 근성으로 피어나

생각이 열리어 오는 오늘
꽃잎을 한 잎씩 뜯으면서
손바닥에 나를 앉힌다.

무언의 손길로 등불을 켤 때
바람결 나의 온기여.

비 오는 산 너머
사라졌던 메아리가
되울릴 수 있다면
나도 또다시 돌아올지 모르지.

발길에 여울지는 것
온통 그을린 눈으로 뒤덮어 놓은 분수일 따름
삭아가는 내부를 안으로만 저울질하며
무언가 되돌리는 깊이로
항시 마중 나갔지.

Greeting the news

Go somewhere and
Blooms into the patience of wildflowers and

Today when the thought is opened and coming
Tearing petals one by one,
Putting me on my palm.

When turning on the lamp with a silent touch
It's my warmth with the wind.

Over the rainy mountain
The disappeared echo,
If it can resonate again
I could come back again.

The abundant thing under my footstep,
It's only my limitation covered with wholly scorched eyes
Weighing only internally the decaying inside,
At the depth of something's return
Always I've gone out to greet it.

초록의 얇은 파문은
어지러움 속으로 다가온다.

청명한 밤
헐리지 않게 받쳐들으면
잊혀진 내가 돌아와 줄지 모르지.

A greenish thinned ripple,
Comes closer dizziness.

The clear night,
If supporting it up not to be broken down,
Maybe I'll come back after I've forgotten.

제 모습 찾기

정년퇴직한 교장 몇이서
고래실 논 삼백여 평 사가지고
황토배기 밭으로 만들어
한 켠에 초막집 치고
소출은 바라지 않는 농사짓기를 한다기에
시골 장터 지나는 길에
보습 하나 사 들고 해거름에 찾아갔더니

비 온 뒤라 인기척도 없고
상추 대궁에 매달린 꽃이
마른 오이 넝쿨에 휘감긴 채
노을 속으로 수줍음을 탄다.

돋보기를 쓰고 세상을 들여다보는데
보이는 건 어른거림일 뿐.

땅거미가 바람 앞세워 성큼 다가와
내 혼자 서 있는 자리에
오늘 하루도 지나쳐 간다.

Finding myself

Heard that some retired principals
Have bought with the fertile rice field about 300 pyeong and
Made it into a red clay farm
Build a thatched hut at one corner
Will farm without expecting crops,
On my way through the country market
Visited there with taking a plowshare after buying it at sunset

Because after the rain, there's no indication of a person
The flowers hung on the stalk of lettuce
Winding on the dried cucumber vine,
Get shy in the glow of sunset.

Looking into the world with a magnifying glass
What I see is only a flicker.

The twilight has already approached putting ahead the wind
Where I stand alone,
Today is passing by.

겨울나무를 대신하여

노을이 풍경소리에 진다.
가녀린 마음이 무엇을
흔들고 있나보다.
눈빛 하나로
흘러간 시간도
흔들 수 있다면
혼란과 모순에 가득 차 있는 나를
흔들고 싶다.

어둠이 되려는 마음만 확인했을 뿐
어둠은 그렇게 돌아오지 않았다.

번뇌 한 자락 흔들어 깨우는
보이지 않는 손길뿐이었다.

On behalf of the winter tree

The sunset falls in the sound of the scenery.
The fragile mind
May sways something.
With one glance
The passed time also
If I can shake it,
I want to shake myself
Filled with confusion and contradictions.

Just confirmed the mind to become darkness but
The darkness didn't come back like that.

Awakening with swaying one edge of anguish,
That was just an invisible touching hand.

달밤의 환영

비에 흠뻑 젖어 되돌아 온
침묵의 끝에 잃어버린 꿈을
호젓이 질퍽이고 있었지.

흘러내린 한밤의 공허
어딘가로 서서히 가라앉고 있었지.

하늬바람으로 떠오르다가
벼랑으로 쏟아져 내리는
나의 모습.

다가갈 수도 없고
다가올 수도 없을
검버섯 핀 얼굴이었지.

겨울 들판을 지나
구름 걸친 기슭이
다가와 머물면
걱정과 걱정이 삭정이같이 떨어지고
달빛 아래
그리움 환하게 열리었지.

Moon night hallucination

Returned as the whole wet from the rain
That lost dream after the end of silence
I made it muddy quietly.

The midnight hollowness that flowed down
Was sinking slowly somewhere.

Soaring as a west wind
Pouring down a precipice,
My appearance.

Unable to approach and
Unable to come,
It was the face with age spots.

Passing the winter field,
The foot of the mountain with wearing the clouds
If it came closer and stay,
The worry and the concerns were falling like brushwood
Under the moonlight
The longings might open brightly.

밤이 안개로 자욱하고
나는 다시 눈을 뜬 꿈결이었지.

The night was full with fog

I was in the dream of opening my eyes again.

제4부 Part 4

사랑과 이별의 물수제비뜨기
The skipping stones of love and farewell

산다는 건
떠밀리며 쏟아지는
꽃씨 같은 것
그 속의 찬바람과
하늘을 다스리는 것.
- 「꽃씨 속 하늘」 중에서

To live is
Being pushing and pouring
Like a floral seed
Controlling the cold wind in it and
The sky inside it.
- The part of 「The sky inside a floral seed」

임에게

텅 빈 몸짓으로
마주 서서
나팔꽃 이슬 톡톡 털며
아침을 나눠 갖게 되었습니다.

무어라 말 다 못했지만
아끼고 다스려
주고받음의
오롯한 흔적으로 남겨 두세요.

어쩌다 새벽이 들깨우면
창문을 열고
입김으로 얼굴을 그려 보세요.

To my beloved

As an empty gesture
Standing face to face
Shaking off the dew of morning glory,
Became to share the morning.

Couldn't have finished saying something, but
Taking care of it and controlling it
Please leave it just as a trace
Of Giving and taking.

Sometimes when the dawn wakes up boisterously
Please open the window and
Draw your face with your breath.

너에게

모든 것을 잊은 채
이슬과 입맞춤한다
너는 나에게 졸음을 안내한다
별들이 내 무릎에 앉아 있는 동안
나는 수없이 굴절된다.

주위는 순백으로 놓여 있다
고요를 포갠 밤하늘이다.

이 잉태의 시공을 아끼고 싶다
모든 게 파묻힌 땅 속에서
민들레가 움 틀 때까지.

삶의 애씀이여
신비의 덫에 치인 나에게도
봄의 몫이 배당되는지

나는 너에게
더딘 성장의 목소리로
지워져 지워져버리고
창조된다.

To you

Forgetting everything
I kiss to dew.
You introduce me to drowsiness
While the stars are sitting on my knees,
I am refracted countlessly.

The surroundings are laid in pure white,
It was the night sky where folds the silence.

I want to save this time and space of this pregnancy
In the ground, where everything is buried,
Until the dandelion sprouts.

The struggle of life, it is!
Even to me who was captivated by a mysterious strap,
Whether spring's share is allocated.

I am, to you
In a slow voice of growth
Erased and erased and
Invented.

양지동 소묘 · 1

일천구백육십이 년 늦가을
나는 제대로 잠자리가 없었다.

쪽마당 멍석 위에서
목화냄새 그득한 이불로
시린 콧등을 가릴 때

아, 마구 쏟아져
출렁대던 은하수.

이제도 그 자리에 누우면
그 때 그 꿈 그대로 남아 있을까.

감출 길 없는 내심은
짐승 같은 눈망울로
하늘이 벙그는 것을 보았다.

내가 나에게
손님으로
꿈을 만들었다.

Yangji-dong Sketch · 1

Late autumn of 1962
I had no proper place to sleep.

On the straw mat in the part of the yard
With the blanket filled with the smell of cotton
When hiding the top of a cold nose,

Ah, pouring out
The swaying Milky Way.

Now again, if I lie there,
Will that dream of those times remain as it is?

The inward mind with no way to hide
With brutal eyes
Saw the sky's beaming.

To myself
As a guest
I made a dream.

양지동 소묘 · 2

마냥 기적소리 아련히 이어질 때
모두가 꿈이던
소년을 호올로이서

비로소
밤이 되었습니다.

그 시절 이후 밤은
나의 전부였습니다.

Yangji-dong Sketch · 2

When the whistle of the train always continues faintly
His dream was everything
A boy, alone

Became
Finally, night.

The night after those years,
It was my everything.

양지동 소묘 · 3

길 건너 산 아래 어둠 속
쬐끄만 가스등
너울너울 나를 부르기에

겁먹은 짐승처럼
한발 한발 다가갔더니

찌그러진 양은그릇
내 형상 같아서
끔벅이던 끔벅이던 빛
빛, 빛, 빛살
번쩍거림뿐이었다.

Yangji-dong Sketch · 3

In the dark under the mountain across the street
A tiny gas lamp
Because it calls me swayingly

Like a scared beast
I went closer step by step

Crushed nickel silverware
It's a like my shape,
Flickering flickering twinkle
Light, light, gleam
It was just a flash.

코스모스

무슨 여한 다시 남겨 놓고 비슷이 서서
하마 무얼 보일 듯 너울대고

이슬 털어 여덟폭 도당치마 여미어
바람자락에 속살 드러내며

이제야 저린 발을 주무르며
소리 없이 서럽다 말하는가.

A cosmos

Leaving some grudges again and standing obliquely,
Flutters as if it shows something and

Brushes off dew and adjusts its mythic skirt of eight in width,
Opens the inner skin by the piece of winds

Only now rubs down its numb feet
Does it say its sadness speechlessly?

꿈 속

유성이 사라지는 하늘
끝에서

어둠을 으깨다 일어났지.

In a dream

The sky where the meteors vanish
At that end

I woke up after crushing the darkness.

꽃이 피어나는 이유

당신의 숨결을
꽉 쥐어짜면
온통 진한 풀물이오.

그 풋내의 언덕으로
홀로 오르며
하늘에 당신을 그리오.

당신이 마구 달려와
어룽진 눈빛으로 허물어지면
비로소 나는 의식을 챙기오.

온 세상의 어둠을 밝히려
모습 내보이는
숨결이오.

The reason why flowers bloom

Your breath
If squeezing it,
It's all thick of grass extract.

To that greenish taste hill
Climbing alone,
I draw you in the sky.

You come running and
If you crumble with a vague glance then
Finally, I manage to care for consciousness.

To lighten the darkness of the whole world
Revealing its appearance,
It's breath.

꽃씨 속 하늘

산다는 건
빨랫줄에 널린 가을을
햇살로 익히는 것.

그늘로 비켜서서
내 고이 간직한 밀어를 불러 모으면
낯선 표정 그대로
악수를 받아 줄 이웃들.

산다는 건
떠밀리며 쏟아지는
꽃씨 같은 것
그 속의 찬바람과
하늘을 다스리는 것.

The sky inside a floral seed

To live is
Ripening the autumn on the clothesline
By sunshine.

Standing aside in the shadow
When I recall together my secret word that is kept carefully,
With the unfamiliar look itself
Neighbors who will take my handshake.

To live is
Being pushing and pouring
Like a floral seed
Controlling the cold wind in it and
The sky inside it,

길에서

착오 없는 질서의 갈피에서

불안한 몸짓의

날개를 접는다.

On the road

In the chasm of order without error

Of anxious gesture

Fold the wings.

거울 속 풍경

거울 앞에선
푸들대는 새가 있어
달빛이 가득하다.

고개를 숙이면
삭이지 못하고 어르는 짐덩이
나만의 심연으로
와르르 쏟아지는 가녘에서마다

눈을 마주하고
기다리는 것
하나부터 빠뜨림 없이
지금은 새로움이다.

무딘 촉수로도
먼 곳의 허욕을 휘둘러보지만

끝내 버릴 수 없는 것으로
되돌아 오고야마는
거울 속의 처음이요
마지막이다.

The scenery in the mirror

In front of the mirror
There's a flickering bird and
The moonlight is full.

When bowing my head,
A bundle of load that is unable to mitigate but calming
Into my abyss
At every clattery pouring edge

With contacting eyes and
Waiting thing,
Without a single omitting
It is new now.

Even with the blunt tentacles,
Swing the vain ambition of a distant place but

As something that can't throw away in the end
There's no choice but to come back,
It's the beginning in the mirror and
The last.

정착지

알 수 없는 죄의
귀양자.
길을 가다가
얼결에 숨을 멈추고
어둠 속을 찾는다.

귀천歸天의 약속이
문지방을 넘어오는 소리.

면도날이 턱을 판다
푸념을 뜯는 장터의 물결은
재액 앞에 선다.

어디에서고 나의 삶은
언제나 부끄럽다.

A settlement area

Of unknown sin
An exile.
On his way
Accidentally holding his breath
Finds the inside of the dark.

The sound that the promise of returning to Heaven
Is crossing the threshold.

The razor blade carves a chin
The wave of the marketplace where it picks complaints,
Stands in front of a misfortune.

Wherever my life is
Always ashamed.

어떤 기다림

지금 이 순간
오랜 밤바다를 지켜보는
안개밭

목쉰 바람이
파도로 다가와 넘실대다가
허황한 한밤을 일깨운다.

미련과 고독의
너울을 바라보는
장승의 하염없는 눈매

안간힘의 몸부림으로
나를 비탈에 세우는 것은
삭일 수 없는 그리움 때문이다
떨쳐버릴 수 없는 그림자 때문이다.

A certain wait

In this moment
Watching the old sea at night,
The fog field

A hoarse wind
Comes as waves and rolling over,
Awakens the hollow midnight.

Of lingering attachment and solitude
Watching the heaving sea,
The totem pole's endless glance

In a desperate struggle
Erecting me on the slope,
It's because of unappeasable longing
It's because of the undetached shadow.

어둠 속의 꿈

서로 변함없는 음색音色으로 닮는다
너울거림은 촉촉한 몸짓으로
푸름의 꽃숲을 닮는다.

번뇌야 무량無量의 달빛으로 씻을 수 있으렷다,
빨랫줄에 널린 바람 한줌
어둠은 실로 소중한 울타리다

낯선 하늘이 내려와
일그러진 손을 잡는다
빛이 어리지 않는 공간에서
모든 두려움의 표정들이
눈빛을 걷어내고
거품 같은 설레임을 걷어낸다

눈부신 고요를 바라본다
나의 빈 곳을
향기로 넘쳐나게 한다

A dream in the dark

Resembling each other as unchangeable tones
The swelling is a moist gesture,
It resembles a greenish flower forest.

The anguish could be washed by infinite moonlight.
A handful of wind hung on the clothesline,
The dark is a really precious fence

An unfamiliar sky comes down,
Grabs my distorted hands
In the space where the light is unreachable
All the scared expressions,
Remove eyeshine and
Remove flutters like a bubble.

Looking at the dazzling tranquility
My empty spot,
I make it full of scents

그대로 수없이 많은 눈길을 외면하면서
산다는 것 그것만으로
아침이고 저녁이고
열어놓은 하늘이고
까맣게 한 점으로
햇살은 굴절되어도
서로가 넘치도록 나눠준다.

Intactly turning away innumerably from many glances,
To live is itself
In the morning and the evening
It's the opened sky and
As a black dot
Even if sunshine is curved,
Shares it fully each other.

그림자 하나 · 2

나의 한 가운데에는
으깨어진 그림자 하나
보라, 기적 소리에 풀과 꽃대궁들이 자지러지는
까슬한 독백을

어둠에 가려진
기다림의 시간을 보낸다.

낭떠러지 위에
숲과 구름과 풍경이 놓인다
도진 두통을 점매고 눕는다.

One shadow · 2

In my center
One crushed shadow
Behold, laughing grasses and flower stalks at whistle sound
That rough monologue

Hidden by the dark,
I am spending the waiting time.

On a precipice
Forest, clouds, and scenery are laid,
Laying down with binding the relapsed headache.

내 이렇게 혼자서

내 이렇게 혼자서
잊고 지낸 숨결에 싸인다.

흩어져 사는 나는
알 수 없는 망상으로 가물거린다
설레임과 떨림이
눈을 감고도 기쁨을 골라낸다.

추억의 모퉁이에 나앉아
더 아름다울 수 있었을 운명과
헛소리도 버리지 않던 모습,
그대여,
나와 같은 허물을 헤집고 있을까.

살아온 사연이야
무슨 바람을 탓하랴만
시린 별빛이 내 발등에 떨어진다.

불꽃으로 피어나
가지마다 움트는 숨소리에 숨어서
나, 다시 돌아오지 않을지 모르지만.

I'm alone like this

I'm alone like this
Surrounded by forgetting breath.

Living dispersed, I am
Flicked with an unknown illusion
The excitement and the trembling,
Collects the joy with closed eyes.

Sitting out in the recollection's corner,
The destiny that could have been more beautiful and
The appearance of not throwing away even drivel,
Dear,
Are you digging up the same faults as me?

The life story is
What kind of wind could I blame for?
But the chilly starlight falls on the top of my feet.

Blooming as fire flake,
Hiding in the breath sound at every sprouting branch
I, don't know if I'll ever come back.

언제나 봄날의 모습으로

모종나무들이 토양에 맞지 않아
시들세라, 신명을 쏟아 부은
사십 성상 외길로
꽂서는 듯 깃듧이 하늘에 치솟아 닿았네.

겸손과 소박의 멋스러운 삶이여.
모습에서부터 은연한 아름다움에 젖어
세상 사는 슬기를 가르치기 으뜸이라.

삼삼한 얼굴들이 눈에 어리시거든
그 자리가 우리 꽃자리임을 잊지 마시고
가르침대로 제 앞가림하도록
흙과 돌을 비집고 뿌리 뻗도록
일손에 젖은 자기 모습이 아득히 보일지라도
엊그제런 듯 서서 웃음 짓고 계십시오.

Always in the springtime

The seedling trees don't fit into the soil, so
Afraid to wither, pouring your body and life
In a single road for forty years of a star,
As if standing upright, the inherent thing soared into the sky.

Wonderful life of humility and simplicity.
Soaked in the subtle beauty from the appearance,
It's the best in teaching the wisdom of living in the world.

If vivid faces are lingering in your eyes,
Don't forget that place is our flower spot,
To take care of ourselves according to the teaching,
So that we can shove aside the soil and stones and take root
Even if you can see yourself wet with your hands,
Please stand and smile as if you were yesterday.

이제껏 닦아 오신 학덕
동행의 지순한 시간이여.
한 올로 펴오르는 사랑의 깊음이여.
빛남이여.

이제 다시 시작하면서
꽃나무들과 어울러 한패가 됐거든
뇌성으로 일러주세요.

지금까지 스승의 뒷모습에도
뜻 세워 산다는 것과 나누고 베푸는 일
한 치 흙 속에도
임이여, 언제나 봄날의 모습으로만 계십시요.

Learning and virtue that you have made efforts
It's entirely pure time to accompany you.
The repayment of love that spreads as one strand.
Splendor, it is!

Now starting over
If you are together with the flower trees,
Please tell us by thunder.

Until now, even in the back of the teacher,
Living up to the will and sharing and giving
Even in a dirt
Beloved, always stay in the springtime.

꽃잎처럼

물감 풀어 허공에
일그러진 자화상을 그린다.

잊을 수도 없도록
살내 나는 달빛과
손목을 잡고

담쑥 쑥대 자라듯
밀려오는 파도,
넘친다는 건
풍요만은 아니다.

노을이 가슴 가득 번진다
스산한 그림자가
몸살을 앓게 한다.

Like petals

Dissolving the paint colors in the air
I draw a twisted self-portrait.

To make it unforgettable
With the moonlight of smelling fresh and
Holding the wrist

As if mugwort stalks grow exuberantly
Incoming waves,
Overflowing is
Not just abundance.

The sunset is spreading fully in my mind
The bleak shadow
Causes my body ache.

鄭松田 시인

- 1962년 「시와 시론」으로 등단.
- 서라벌예술대학 문예창작과 졸.
- 중앙대학교 국문과 및 동 대학원 졸.
- 용인시 죽전중학교 교장, 한라대학교, 경기대학교 겸임교수 역임.
- 세계시문학회 회장 역임.
- 한국자유시인협회 본상, 세계시문학상 대상, 경기도문학상 대상, 경기예술 대상, 현대 시인상 수상.
- 한국현대시인협회 지도위원, 한국작가협회 최고위원.
- 한국현대시인협회, 세계시문학회, 미당 시맥회 회원.

■ 시집
「그리움의 무게」, 「바람의 침묵」, 「꽃과 바람」, 「빛의 울림을 그린다」, 「내 이렇게 살다가」, 「바람의 말」.

■ 자작시 감상 선집
「그리움과 사랑의 되풀이」, 「자연과 우주의 너울」, 「내 삶의 소용돌이」, 「내 인생의 뒤안길」.

■ 한영시집
「숨은 꽃」, 「너를 맞아 보낸다」, 「꽃과 아내」, 「너와의 걸음걸이」

Poet Song-jun Jung

- Debuted with 「Poems and Poetics」 in 1962
- Graduated Literary Creation from Seorabeol University of Arts
- Received and graduated master's degree from Joong-ang University
- School president of Jukjeon Middle School in Yong-in City. Served as affiliated professor of Hanla University and Kyeongki University
- Served as the president of Literary Society of the World Poetry
- Awardee of Korea Free Poet Association, first line up at World Poetry Literature Award, first line up at Kyeonggido Literature Award, first line up at Kyeonggi Art Award, the receipient of the Modern Poet Award.
- Direction committee of Korea Modern Poet Association, the executive committee of Korea Author Association
- Member of Korea Modern Poset Association, World Poet Literary Society, and Midang Poet Line Association

- **Collections of Poems**
  「The weight of longing」, 「The silence of the wind」, 「Flower and wind」, 「Drawing the echo of lights」, 「Iliving in such way」, 「The words of the wind」.

- **Collection of poems for appreciation**
  「Repetition of longing and love」, 「The swell of nature and universe」, 「Whirlpool of my life」, 「Backwaters of my life」.

- **Korean-English Poems**
  「The hidden flower」, 「Sending you after meeting you」, 「Flowers and my wife」, 「Walking with you」

정송전 한영시집 3
꽃과 아내

2022년 8월 18일 1판 1쇄 인쇄
2022년 8월 22일 1판 1쇄 발행

지은이 | 정송전
펴낸이 | 김효열

펴낸곳 | 을지출판공사

등록번호 | 1985년 2월 14일 제2-741호
주　　소 | 서울시 마포구 양화진길 41, 603호
우편번호 | 04083
대표전화 | 02) 334-4050
팩시밀리 | 02) 334-4010
전자우편 | ejp4050@hanmail.net

값 12,000원

ISBN 978-89-7566-216-4　　03810

Korean-English Poems Collection of Jeong Song Jeon 3
Flowers and my wife

1st edition printed August 18, 2022
1st edition published August 22, 2022

Author   Jeong Song Jeon
Publisher   Kim Hyo Yeol

Published   EulJi Publishing Company

Registration 1985. 2. 14 No. 2-741
Address 603. 41, Yanghwajin-gil, Mapo-go, Seoul, Korea
Phone 02-334-4050   Fax 02-334-4010
e-mail ejp4050@hanmail.net

Value 12,000 won

ISBN 978-89-7566-216-4   03810